PRINCETON STUDIES IN INTERNATIONAL FINANCE

No. 76, September 1994

ONE MONEY OR MANY?
ANALYZING THE PROSPECTS FOR MONETARY
UNIFICATION IN VARIOUS PARTS OF THE WORLD

TAMIM BAYOUMI

AND

BARRY EICHENGREEN

D0840514

INTERNATIONAL FINANCE SECTION

DEPARTMENT OF ECONOMICS
PRINCETON UNIVERSITY
PRINCETON, NEW JERSEY

PRINCETON STUDIES
IN INTERNATIONAL FINANCE

PRINCETON STUDIES IN INTERNATIONAL FINANCE are published by the International Finance Section of the Department of Economics of Princeton University. Although the Section sponsors the Studies, the authors are free to develop their topics as they wish. The Section welcomes the submission of manuscripts for publication in this and its other series. Please see the Notice to Contributors at the back of this Study.

The authors of this Study are Tamim Bayoumi and Barry Eichengreen. Tamim Bayoumi is an economist at the Research Department of the International Monetary Fund and has published a number of articles in the fields of international finance and macroeconomics. Barry Eichengreen is John L. Simpson Professor of Economics and Professor of Political Science at the University of California at Berkeley. He is, most recently, the author of *International Monetary Arrangements for the 21st Century* (1994). This is his third contribution to the publications of the International Finance Section.

PETER B. KENEN, *Director*
International Finance Section

PRINCETON STUDIES IN INTERNATIONAL FINANCE

No. 76, September 1994

ONE MONEY OR MANY?
ANALYZING THE PROSPECTS FOR MONETARY
UNIFICATION IN VARIOUS PARTS OF THE WORLD

TAMIM BAYOUMI

AND

BARRY EICHENGREEN

INTERNATIONAL FINANCE SECTION

DEPARTMENT OF ECONOMICS
PRINCETON UNIVERSITY
PRINCETON, NEW JERSEY

INTERNATIONAL FINANCE SECTION
EDITORIAL STAFF

Peter B. Kenen, *Director*

Margaret B. Riccardi, *Editor*

Lillian Spais, *Editorial Aide*

Lalitha H. Chandra, *Subscriptions and Orders*

HG
3894
B39
1994

Library of Congress Cataloging-in-Publication Data

Bayoumi, Tamim A.
   One money or many? : analyzing the prospects for monetary unification in various parts of the world / Tamim Bayoumi and Barry Eichengreen.
      p. cm. — (Princeton studies in international finance, ISSN 0081-8070 ; no. 76)
   Includes bibliographical references.
   ISBN 0-88165-248-2 (pbk.) : $11.00
   1. Monetary unions. 2. Monetary policy. I. Eichengreen, Barry J. II. Title. III. Series.
HG3894.B39 1994
332.4′566—dc20   94-22966
                                                                                              CIP

Printed in the United States of America by Princeton University Printing Services at Princeton, New Jersey

International Standard Serial Number: 0081-8070
International Standard Book Number: 0-88165-248-2
Library of Congress Catalog Card Number: 94-22966

CONTENTS

FIGURE

TABLES

1 INTRODUCTION

Recent years have witnessed a number of developments that have the potential to transform national and international monetary arrangements. The Maastricht Treaty is an important step toward the adoption of a single European currency by at least some members of the European Union (EU).[1] Political disintegration in the former Soviet Union, Yugoslavia, and Czechoslovakia, spelling the end to three existing currency unions, is a significant step in the other direction. Looking into the future, the move toward regionally based free-trade areas in North America, East Asia, and South America may eventually prompt policymakers in these regions, as in Europe, to contemplate the creation of single regional currencies.[2]

These developments have rekindled interest in the literature on optimum currency areas initiated by Mundell in 1961. In Mundell's framework, the gains from monetary unification and a common currency stem from lower transaction costs and the elimination of exchange-rate variability. Losses come from the inability to pursue independent monetary policies and to use the exchange rate as an instrument of adjustment. The magnitude of the losses depends on the incidence of disturbances and the speed with which the economy adjusts. If disturbances and responses are similar across regions, symmetrical policy responses will suffice, eliminating the need for policy autonomy. Only if disturbances are asymmetrically distributed across countries or if speeds of adjustment are markedly different will distinctive national macroeconomic policies be needed and the constraints of monetary union be a hindrance.

Part of the research for this paper was completed while Tamim Bayoumi was at the Bank of England and Barry Eichengreen was at the Federal Reserve Board. Financial support for Barry Eichengreen was provided by the Center for German and European Studies of the University of California at Berkeley. The views expressed in this study are solely the authors', however, and do not necessarily represent those of the above institutions or of the International Monetary Fund.

[1] Formerly called European Community (EC).
[2] For a detailed discussion of regional trading arrangements in these areas, see Torre and Kelly (1992).

1

Disturbances and responses are not, of course, the only factors influencing the choice of international monetary arrangements. Mundell (1961) emphasized the importance of factor mobility for facilitating adjustment. McKinnon (1963) argued that the gains from unification were likely to be an increasing function of the openness of the constituent economies to intraregional trade (because openness magnifies the gains associated with the reductions of the transaction costs). And Kenen (1969) proposed that the diversification of the economy should be used to assess the appropriateness of a currency area, arguing that highly diversified economies are less likely to experience the sort of asymmetric shocks that independent exchange rates are useful for offsetting.

Several recent studies investigate the incidence of disturbances as a way of analyzing the suitability of different groups of nations for monetary union. Many of these studies focus on Europe, where the issue has particular immediacy, and some compare the variability of relative prices in the EU with those in existing monetary unions like the United States and Canada (Poloz, 1990; Eichengreen, 1992; De Grauwe and Vanhaverbeke, 1993). A limitation of this approach is that the movement of relative prices conflates the effects of disturbances and responses; it is not possible to identify the relevant structural parameters on the basis of the behavior of such semi-reduced-form variables. Some other studies consider the behavior of output itself, attempting to distinguish common from idiosyncratic national shocks (Cohen and Wyplosz, 1989; Weber, 1991). These studies compute sums and differences in output movements for groups of European countries, interpreting the sums as symmetric disturbances and the differences as asymmetric disturbances. The problem with this approach is that output movements are not the same as shocks; they, too, conflate information on disturbances and responses. This strategy also fails to distinguish between disturbances emanating from different sources, such as impulses to demand related to the conduct of monetary and fiscal policies as against shifts in supply associated with the shocks to the real economy.

The present study uses a structural vector-autoregression approach developed by Blanchard and Quah (1989) to identify aggregate supply and demand disturbances and to distinguish them from subsequent responses.[3] These measures can be used to identify groups of countries

---

[3] The authors used this approach previously in a series of related papers to analyze Economic and Monetary Union (EMU), the possible extension of EMU to the European Free Trade Association (EFTA) countries, and the North American Free Trade Agreement (NAFTA), respectively (Bayoumi and Eichengreen, 1993, 1994a, 1995).

suited for monetary union. The estimated disturbances point to more clear-cut groupings than the time series on output and the prices from which they are derived. Vector autoregression identifies three sets of countries that, on the basis of their macroeconomic disturbances and responses, are plausible candidates for monetary unification: a Northern European group comprised of Germany and a subset of other potential participants in EMU (Austria, Belgium, Denmark, France, the Netherlands, and perhaps Switzerland); a Northeast Asian bloc (Japan, Korea, and Taiwan); and a Southeast Asian area (Hong Kong, Indonesia, Malaysia, Singapore, and possibly Thailand). Notably absent from this list are countries in either North or South America.

To provide a context in which to interpret our results, Chapter 2 presents a selective survey of the literature on optimum currency areas. Chapters 3 and 4 describe the methodology we used to distinguish disturbances and adjustment dynamics and the data employed in the analysis. Chapters 5 and 6 report our estimates and discuss their implications. Chapter 7 presents, for comparison, results using regional data for the United States, an existing monetary union. Chapter 8 concludes the study.

2 OPTIMUM CURRENCY AREAS

This chapter selectively surveys the literature on optimum currency areas and highlights aspects and ambiguities of that inquiry relevant to the analysis presented below. For more comprehensive surveys, the reader may consult Ishiyama (1975) or Tavlas (1992).

Mundell, in his seminal contribution, emphasized two criteria pertinent to deciding whether to abandon policy autonomy for a monetary union: the nature of disturbances and the ease of response. We consider them in turn.

Nature of Disturbances

If two regions experience the same disturbances, they will presumably favor the same policy responses.[1] Abandoning policy autonomy for monetary unification will then entail relatively little cost. It is curious that the magnitude of disturbances, as opposed to their correlation, has received little attention in the literature. Consider a set of disturbances that are negatively correlated across a pair of countries. If those disturbances are of negligible size, the two countries may still incur only minor costs from forsaking policy autonomy because output, unemployment and other relevant variables will barely be disturbed from their equilibrium levels. Clearly, discussions of monetary unification focusing on the nature of disturbances should consider their size as well as their cross-country correlation.

Subsequent to Mundell, the literature has followed Kenen (1969) in linking structural characteristics of economies—and, in particular, the sectoral composition of production—to the characteristics of shocks. This literature suggests that economies sharing the same industries are likely to experience similar aggregate disturbances insofar as economy-wide disturbances are the aggregates of industry-specific shocks. If disturbances are imperfectly correlated across industries, diversified economies may experience smaller aggregate disturbances than will highly specialized economies. In particular, if two economies specialize in sectors that respectively produce and use primary products, there is

---

[1] Strictly speaking, this assumes that preferences in the two countries are the same. Corden (1972) suggests that differences in preferences across countries can also obstruct movement toward monetary union.

good reason to anticipate that the disturbances they experience will be negatively correlated.

Ease of Response

If market mechanisms adjust smoothly and restore equilibrium rapidly, asymmetric disturbances need not imply significant costs for entities denied the option of an independent policy response. Even large shocks that displace macroeconomic variables from normal levels will have relatively small costs if the initial equilibrium is restored quickly. Mundell focused on labor mobility as an adjustment mechanism. If asymmetric shocks raising unemployment in one region relative to another elicit labor flows from the former to the latter, unemployment may return to normal levels before significant costs have been incurred even if the authorities lack policy instruments to expedite adjustment. Blanchard and Katz (1992) have recently affirmed the importance of this mechanism in the United States. Interregional migration contributes more to internal adjustment in the United States than do changes in either relative wages or labor-force participation rates. It is clear from the work of Blanchard and Katz, however, that migration is but one of several channels through which adjustment to asymmetric shocks can occur. Equilibrium is also restored through adjustments in relative wages (upward in regions experiencing positive shocks, downward in others), by the changes in labor-force participation induced by these wage changes, and by capital mobility into those regions experiencing temporary negative disturbances. Blanchard and Katz conclude, however, that, for the United States, the Mundellian assumption that labor mobility is the principal channel for adjustment is broadly consistent with the facts. They also identify differences across regions in the importance of the different adjustment mechanisms. In the U.S. manufacturing belt, for example, relatively little adjustment occurs through changes in relative wages.

Whether potential monetary unions in other parts of the world display comparable labor mobility is questionable. The Organisation for Economic Co-operation and Development (OECD, 1987) provides tabulations indicating that French and German workers are only a third as likely to move between *départements* and *lander* as Americans are to move between states. According to migration equations reported in Eichengreen (1993), the elasticity of interregional migratory flows with respect to internal wage and unemployment differentials is smaller in Great Britain and Italy than in the United States. Guest workers from Turkey and other sources outside the EU may be more mobile and responsive to changes in economic conditions, but, in many countries, their impact on destination labor markets is limited to unskilled jobs and the informal sector. Goto and Hamada (1994) point to the extent of labor mobility in Asia, where countries like Singapore have a larger share of immigrants in their labor force than has any industrial country but Switzerland. Other countries like Japan and South Korea, however, are less accommodating of guest workers.

Implication for Policy

The implication for policy is that countries experiencing large asymmetric disturbances are poor candidates for forming a monetary union, because these are the countries where policy autonomy has the greatest utility. Indeed, this is the implication we use in this paper to interpret our empirical results. Before proceeding, however, it is worth noting several qualifications.

First, even if countries experience large, asymmetric disturbances, it need not follow that policy autonomy is useful for facilitating adjustment. If money is neutral, it will not help to offset disturbances to output. Most of the recent literature on monetary policy, however, though written by authors approaching the question from very different perspectives, does support the view that monetary initiatives affect relative prices and quantities (for example, Romer and Romer, 1989; Eichenbaum and Evans, 1993). In models with coordination failure, nominal contracting, and other sources of inertia, monetary policy can speed adjustment whether the disturbance in question is a supply shock that permanently shifts the long-run equilibrium or a demand shock that temporarily displaces output and prices from invariant steady-state levels.

Second, even countries that value policy autonomy may be willing to abandon monetary independence if they retain other flexible policy instruments, of which fiscal policy is the obvious candidate. In monetary unions like the United States, state and local governments run budget deficits in periods of recession and accumulate nonnegligible debts. In 1990, the ratio of state debt to gross state product averaged 2.4 percent.[2] In practice, the high mobility of capital and labor in a monetary union constrains the fiscal flexibility of constituent jurisdictions. If mobile factors of production are able to flee the taxes needed to service heavy debt burdens, governments may find themselves unable to finance budget deficits by borrowing in capital markets cognizant of this

---

[2] Many states impose statutory and constitutional limits on their ability to borrow; see below and in Bayoumi and Eichengreen (1994b).

6

constraint on the authorities' capacity to tax. Bayoumi and Eichengreen (1994b) estimate that state governments in the United States, which operate in an environment of high factor mobility, find themselves rationed out of the capital market when their debt-to-income ratios approach 9 percent. In addition, worries that participants in a monetary union will free-ride by issuing debt in excess of their ability to service it, forcing other members to bail out them out, has led the architects of the CFA franc zone and the EU's prospective monetary union to adopt statutes designed to limit the fiscal autonomy of constituent jurisdictions. Finally, there is the fact that, for political reasons, fiscal policy is less easily adapted than monetary policy to changing economic conditions. For all these reasons, fiscal policy is likely to be an imperfect substitute for the abandoned monetary instrument.

A third qualification is that policymakers may systematically misuse policy rather than employ it to facilitate adjustment. For countries that succumb repeatedly to high inflation, for example, it is hard to argue that forsaking monetary-policy autonomy is costly. One interpretation of asymmetrically distributed aggregate demand shocks is that the countries concerned are poor candidates for monetary union, because policymakers can use demand-management instruments to offset demand shocks emanating from other sources. But, if domestic policy itself is the source of the disturbances, monetary unification with a group of countries less susceptible to such pressures may imply a welfare improvement.

A fourth and final qualification is that the nature of disturbances across a group of countries may be correlated with other characteristics that also affect their suitability for participation in a monetary union. Take, for instance, Kenen's point that a high degree of specialization in production is likely to be associated with asymmetric shocks and therefore with floating exchange rates between separate currencies. A high degree of specialization also implies that floating exchange rates may be very disruptive of living standards. Fixing the value of the national currency in terms of a country's dominant export commodity—this being the implication of adopting a floating rate—will subject households to fluctuations in their purchasing power. These households may prefer that the government insure them against purchasing-power fluctuations by stabilizing the value of the currency in terms of some broader aggregation of goods, that is, by fixing the exchange rate or by joining a monetary union. In practice, a high degree of specialization appears to be one of the strongest empirical correlates of the decision to peg the exchange rate (see, for example, the evidence provided by Honkapohja and Pikkarainen, 1992).

3 METHODOLOGY

In describing the methodology used to estimate aggregate supply and demand disturbances, our point of departure is the familiar diagram reproduced as the top panel of Figure 1. The short-run aggregate supply curve (SRAS) is upward sloping under the assumption that capacity utilization can be varied in the short run to exploit the profit opportunities afforded by changes in aggregate demand. The long-run aggregate supply curve (LRAS) is vertical, because capacity utilization eventually returns to normal, preventing demand shocks from permanently affecting the level of production. The aggregate demand curve (AD) is downward sloping in price-output space, reflecting the fact that lower prices raise real-money balances and therefore product demand.

Now consider the effects of permanent aggregate supply and demand shocks. The effect of a positive demand shock is shown in the left half of the lower panel. As the aggregate demand curve shifts from AD to AD′, the short-run equilibrium moves from its initial point E to the intersection of SRAS with AD′, and output and prices rise. As the aggregate supply curve becomes increasingly vertical over time, the economy moves gradually from the short-run equilibrium D′ to the long-run equilibrium D″. The economy traverses the new aggregate demand curve, output falls back to its initial level, and the price level continues to rise. The response to a positive demand shock is a short-run rise in production followed by a gradual return to the initial level of output, and a permanent rise in prices.

The effects of a positive supply disturbance (such as a favorable technology shock) that permanently raises potential output is shown in the right-hand bottom panel. The short- and long-run aggregate supply curves shift to the right by the same amount, displacing the short-run equilibrium from E to S′. On impact, output rises and prices fall. As the supply curve becomes increasingly vertical over time, the economy moves from S′ to S″, leading to further increases in output and additional declines in prices. Whereas outward shifts in the aggregate demand curve, though permanent, affect output only temporarily, outward shifts in the aggregate supply curve affect output permanently. And, whereas positive demand shocks raise prices, positive supply shocks reduce them.

FIGURE 1
THE AGGREGATE SUPPLY AND DEMAND MODEL

The Model

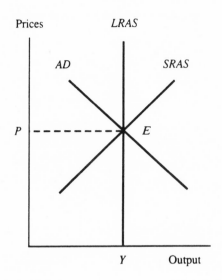

A Demand Shock   A Supply Shock

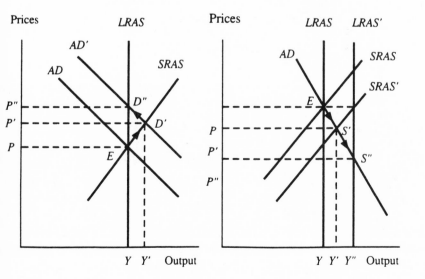

External as well as internal disturbances are readily incorporated into the framework of aggregate supply and demand. Consider, for example, a rise in oil prices. For oil-importing countries, such a disturbance should be treated first and foremost as a supply shock. The change in the relative price of inputs lowers the value of the existing capital stock, reducing the equilibrium level of output. But there are also negative repercussions on demand owing to the adverse movement in the terms of trade. This, however, is not likely to be large in the case of oil-importing countries, because the proportion of total demand that is associated with oil consumption is relatively small. The impact on aggregate demand is therefore likely to be swamped by the macro-economic policy response to the oil-price shock.

The same need not be true for countries where output is dominated by production of oil (or other raw materials). In those countries, a change in relative prices is likely to show up as both an aggregate supply disturbance and an aggregate demand disturbance. A rise in oil prices is likely to affect Indonesia, for example, both by raising the underlying level of output through the increased incentive to produce oil and by boosting aggregate demand through the favorable impact of the terms of trade on real incomes. Hence, for producers of oil, it may be difficult to distinguish between the aggregate supply and demand disturbances caused by a change in oil prices.

We estimate our model using a procedure proposed by Blanchard and Quah (1989) for distinguishing temporary from permanent shocks to a pair of time-series variables; it was extended to the present case by Bayoumi (1992). Consider a system in which the true model can be represented by an infinite moving average of a (vector) of variables X_t and an equal number of shocks ε_t. Using the lag operator L, this can be written as

$$
\begin{aligned}
X_t &= A_0 \varepsilon_t + A_1 \varepsilon_{t-1} + A_2 \varepsilon_{t-2} + A_3 \varepsilon_{t-3} \cdots \\
&= \sum_{i=0}^{\infty} L^i A_i \varepsilon_t ,
\end{aligned}
\tag{1}
$$

where the matrices A_i represent the impulse response functions of the shocks to the elements of X.

Specifically, let X_t be made up of change in output and the change in prices, and let ε_t be supply and demand shocks. Then, the model becomes

$$
\begin{bmatrix} \Delta y_t \\ \Delta p_t \end{bmatrix} = \sum_{i=0}^{\infty} L^i \begin{bmatrix} a_{11i} & a_{12i} \\ a_{21i} & a_{22i} \end{bmatrix} \begin{bmatrix} \varepsilon_{dt} \\ \varepsilon_{st} \end{bmatrix} ,
\tag{2}
$$

where y_t and p_t represent the logarithm of output and prices, a_{11i} represents element a_{11} in matrix A_i, and ε_{dt} and ε_{st} are independent supply and demand shocks. The two shocks will be independent if they have separate causes, such as shifts in macroeconomic policy in the case of aggregate demand disturbances and technological innovations in the case of aggregate supply disturbances. If, however, the same underlying disturbance causes movements in both cases—for example, a change in commodity prices for a commodity producer—this identification will break down. The estimated aggregate supply disturbance in this case will incorporate the associated effect on aggregate demand (see further discussion below).

This framework implies that, although supply shocks have permanent effects on the level of output, demand shocks have only temporary effects (though both have permanent effects on the level of prices). Because output is written in first-difference form, the cumulative effect of demand shocks on the change in output (Δy_t) must be zero. This implies the restriction

$$\sum_{i-0}^{\infty} a_{11i} = 0 . \tag{3}$$

The model defined by equations (2) and (3) can be estimated using a vector autoregression. As in any vector autoregression, each element of X_t is regressed on lagged values of all the elements of X. Using B to represent these estimated coefficients, the vector autoregression can be written in matrix form as

$$\begin{aligned} X_t &= B_1 X_{t-1} + B_2 X_{t-2} + \ldots + B_n X_{t-n} + e_t \\ &= [I - B(L)]^{-1} e_t \\ &= [I + B(L) + B(L)^2 + \ldots] e_t \\ &= e_t + D_1 e_{t-1} + D_2 e_{t-2} + D_3 e_{t-3} + \ldots , \end{aligned} \tag{4}$$

where e_t represents the residuals from the equations in the vector autoregression. In the case being considered, X_t is comprised of Δy_t and Δp_t, and e_t is comprised of the residuals of a regression of lagged values of Δy_t and Δp_t on current values of each in turn; these residuals are labeled e_{yt} and e_{pt}, respectively.

To convert equation (4) into the model defined by equations (2) and (3), the residuals from the vector autoregression (e_t) must be transformed into supply and demand (ε_t). Writing $e_t = C\varepsilon_t$, in the two-by-two case considered, four restrictions are required to define the four elements of the matrix C. Two of these restrictions are simple normali-

11

zations, which define the variance of the shocks ε_{dt} and ε_{st}. A third restriction comes from assuming that supply and demand shocks are orthogonal.

The final restriction, which allows the matrix C to be uniquely defined, is that demand shocks have only temporary effects on output. As noted above, this implies equation (3). In terms of the vector autoregression,

$$\sum_{i=0}^{\infty} \begin{bmatrix} d_{11i} & d_{12i} \\ d_{21i} & d_{22i} \end{bmatrix} \begin{bmatrix} c_{11} & c_{12} \\ c_{21} & c_{22} \end{bmatrix} = \begin{bmatrix} 0 & . \\ . & . \end{bmatrix}. \tag{5}$$

This restriction allows the matrix C to be uniquely defined and the supply and demand shocks to be identified.[1]

Clearly, it is controversial to interpret shocks with a permanent impact on output as supply disturbances and shocks with a temporary impact on output as demand disturbances. Doing so implies adopting the battery of assumptions implicit in the model of aggregate supply and demand of Figure 1. One can think of frameworks other than the standard aggregate supply and demand model in which that association breaks down. It is conceivable that temporary supply shocks (for example, an oil-price increase that is subsequently reversed) or demand shocks with permanent effects on real variables (for example, a permanent increase in government spending) dominate our data. Here, a critical feature of our methodology comes into play. Although restriction (5) defines the response of output to the two shocks, it says nothing about the response of prices. The aggregate supply and demand model predicts that positive demand shocks should raise prices, whereas positive supply shocks should lower them. Because these responses are not imposed, they can be thought of as "over-identifying restrictions" useful for testing our interpretation of permanent output disturbances in terms of supply and temporary output disturbances in terms of demand. In other words, the impulse-response functions can be used to test directly the validity of our structural interpretation of the vector autoregression.

We find that the restriction is satisfied for most of the countries studied. However, several countries that are heavily dependent on raw-material production fail to satisfy the prediction of a negative price

---

[1] Note from equation (4) that the long-run impact of the shocks on output and prices is equal to $[I - B(1)]^{-1}$. The restriction that the long-run effect of demand shocks on output is zero implies a simple linear restriction on the coefficients of this matrix.

12

response to permanent disturbances. As discussed earlier, this probably reflects the fact that, for raw-material producers, positive supply shocks are associated with increases in the relative price of raw materials (improvements in the terms of trade) and, hence, with positive aggregate demand shocks. For such countries, "supply shocks" also have aggregate demand effects, producing the perverse behavior of prices.[2] Some evidence consistent with this interpretation is presented below.

This vector-autoregressive methodology is clearly not the only approach that might be taken to identify the pattern of disturbances. One alternative is to impose fewer assumptions and to identify disturbances to output and prices with movements in those same variables. Authors like Baxter and Stockman (1989) proceed essentially in this fashion. At the other extreme lie large-scale stochastic simulations of multicountry macroeconomic models like those in Bryant (1993). The advantage of the vector-autoregressive methodology is that it provides a simple and intuitive method of identifying the underlying macroeconomic disturbances using the closest thing to a consensus model in the macroeconomics literature. Readers who consider the first approach too atheoretical and the second as burdened by too many maintained assumptions are likely to prefer the middle ground we stake out here.

[2] This mismeasurement only affects aggregate demand disturbances that are associated with the terms of trade. Other disturbances, such as those associated with macroeconomic policy, should still be measured correctly.

4 DATA

Annual data on real and nominal gross domestic product (GDP) were collected for three regions: Western Europe (hereafter Europe), East Asia (hereafter Asia) and the Americas. The European data cover fifteen countries, ten members of the EU plus the five members of EFTA.[1] Eleven Asian economies were studied, including all the members of the Association of Southeast Asian Nations (ASEAN) except Brunei, plus Australia and New Zealand, with which ASEAN has a free-trade agreement.[2] Thirteen countries were considered in the Americas, including the three nations involved in NAFTA and the members of the Southern Cone Common Market (MERCOSUR).[3] For each of these economies, an attempt was made to assemble consistent data for as long a period as possible. The European data are drawn from the OECD's *Annual National Accounts* and span the period from 1960 to 1990. For Asia (except Taiwan) and the Americas, the data come from the World Bank publications and cover the somewhat shorter period from 1969 to 1989. Data for Taiwan are drawn from national sources.

Before estimating and analyzing supply and demand disturbances, we considered the data directly. Table 1 reports the mean and standard deviation of growth (measured as the change in the logarithm of real output) and inflation (the change in the logarithm of the GDP deflator) for each economy, along with regional averages. Because growth and inflation are measured as the change in the logarithm of real GDP and of the GDP deflator, respectively, a value of 0.01 represents a change of roughly 1 percent.

The simple averages highlight the high rates of growth achieved over the last twenty years in Asia and the high levels of inflation

---

[1] The full set of European countries includes Austria, Belgium, Denmark, Finland, France, Germany, Ireland, Italy, the Netherlands, Norway, Portugal, Spain, Sweden, Switzerland, and the United Kingdom. Luxembourg was excluded because of its small size and Greece, because of its eastern location. The same methodology can be applied to Greece and yields sensible results (Bayoumi and Eichengreen, 1993).

[2] This group includes Australia, Hong Kong, Indonesia, Japan, Korea, Malaysia, New Zealand, the Philippines, Singapore, Taiwan, and Thailand.

[3] This set includes Argentina, Bolivia, Brazil, Canada, Chile, Colombia, Ecuador, Mexico, Paraguay, Peru, the United States, Uruguay, and Venezuela.

14

TABLE 1
BASIC STATISTICS OF DIFFERENT GEOGRAPHIC REGIONS

	Growth		Inflation	
	Mean	Standard Deviation	Mean	Standard Deviation
Western Europe				
Austria	0.034	0.020	0.045	0.018
Belgium	0.032	0.021	0.051	0.024
Denmark	0.027	0.023	0.072	0.024
Finland	0.037	0.023	0.081	0.036
France	0.034	0.017	0.068	0.031
Germany	0.029	0.022	0.039	0.016
Ireland	0.040	0.022	0.086	0.052
Italy	0.036	0.023	0.098	0.053
Netherlands	0.032	0.022	0.051	0.028
Norway	0.037	0.018	0.065	0.033
Portugal	0.044	0.033	0.122	0.072
Spain	0.041	0.026	0.102	0.043
Sweden	0.027	0.018	0.072	0.026
Switzerland	0.024	0.026	0.044	0.022
United Kingdom	0.024	0.021	0.081	0.051
Average	0.033	0.022	0.072	0.035
East Asia				
Australia	0.031	0.019	0.094	0.029
Hong Kong	0.080	0.046	0.085	0.038
Indonesia	0.062	0.023	0.147	0.103
Japan	0.043	0.020	0.045	0.047
Korea	0.085	0.038	0.122	0.078
Malaysia	0.066	0.033	0.046	0.060
New Zealand	0.025	0.042	0.086	0.059
Philippines	0.037	0.045	0.127	0.091
Singapore	0.075	0.034	0.042	0.044
Taiwan	0.083	0.035	0.066	0.070
Thailand	0.070	0.031	0.067	0.051
Average	0.060	0.033	0.084	0.061
The Americas				
Argentina	0.006	0.043	1.184	0.771
Bolivia	0.016	0.038	0.746	1.194
Brazil	0.051	0.048	0.809	0.661
Canada	0.038	0.023	0.067	0.031
Chile	0.023	0.075	0.581	0.610
Colombia	0.043	0.020	0.211	0.034
Ecuador	0.056	0.069	0.217	0.148
Mexico	0.040	0.041	0.340	0.233
Paraguay	0.058	0.045	0.165	0.076
Peru	0.015	0.065	0.697	0.776
United States	0.028	0.025	0.058	0.024
Uruguay	0.016	0.045	0.476	0.127
Venezuela	0.015	0.043	0.159	0.156
Average	0.031	0.045	0.439	0.372

prevalent in Latin America. The standard deviations suggest significant regional differences, with Europe displaying the most stable growth and inflation rates, followed by Asia and the Americas.[4] There are pronounced variations within groups: the United States and Canada behave differently than the rest of the Americas; Japan and Australia behave differently than the rest of Asia.

Tables 2 and 3 report correlation coefficients between GDP growth and inflation, respectively, for each of our three regions. European growth rates fall into three groups. A core of five countries (Austria, Belgium, France, Germany, and the Netherlands) have growth rates that are highly correlated both within the group and with other European countries; an intermediate group of six countries (Finland, Italy, Portugal, Spain, Sweden, and Switzerland) have relatively high correlations with the aforementioned core countries and with their immediate neighbors, but not with other European countries; and a third group (Finland, Ireland, Norway, and the United Kingdom) have relatively idiosyncratic output fluctuations. In contrast, cross-country correlations of European inflation rates do not suggest the existence of clearly defined country groupings.[5]

The Asian economies exhibit less coherent output fluctuations than those in Europe show, although two overlapping subregions with relatively high correlations can be distinguished, one comprised of Hong Kong, Japan, Singapore, and Taiwan, the other including Hong Kong, Indonesia, Malaysia, and Singapore. Unlike Europe, however, inflation rates in Asia display a distinct regional pattern. Australia, Japan, Korea, Singapore, Taiwan, and Thailand exhibit high intercountry inflation correlations, as do Hong Kong, Indonesia, Malaysia, Singapore, and Thailand.

Growth and inflation correlations for the Americas are shown in the bottom panel of Tables 2 and 3. Although U.S. and Canadian output growth rates are correlated, as expected, the correlations between these two countries and Mexico, the third nation involved in the NAFTA negotiations, are far from high. Mexican inflation is negatively correlated with that of the other two countries. The same pattern holds between

---

[4] This conclusion is dependent on the standardization of the variation in European growth rates for the region's lower mean growth rate. When the variability of the growth rates is measured by coefficients of variation, European growth rates are somewhat less stable than those of Asia over the sample period.

[5] In particular, Finland, Ireland, Norway, and the United Kingdom are not so obviously atypical from the perspective of inflation as they are from that of output.

the United States and the South American countries, with growth being positively correlated and inflation negatively correlated. Within South America, the output data reveal two overlapping country groups with reasonably high correlations within each group. One includes Brazil, Colombia, Ecuador, Peru, and Venezuela; the other, Bolivia, Brazil, Paraguay, and Uruguay. Inflation shows a different pattern, with high-inflation countries like Argentina, Brazil, Peru, and somewhat more surprisingly, Ecuador and Venezuela, displaying higher cross-correlations than the other countries.

When assessing the significance of these correlations, it is desirable to exclude that part accounted for by the international business cycle, for only deviations from common movements are important in assessing the suitability of a group of countries for monetary unification. Correlations between output growth and inflation in the Group of Three (G-3) countries—Germany, Japan, and the United States—were used as the basis for our choice of the underlying correlation. In both cases, the correlations between these countries were approximately 0.5, so 0.5 was used as the null hypothesis. This implies a critical value for positive correlations of 0.74.[6]

This criterion highlights a limited number of significant correlations.[7] Although over half the correlations of output growth rates between Austria, Belgium, France, Germany, and the Netherlands are significant, growth rates for the rest of the economies shown in Table 2 yield only five significant correlations, one of which is between the United States and Canada. Europe shows no pattern of significant correlations for inflation (Table 3), but a distinct regional pattern does emerge in Asia, where Japan, Korea, and Taiwan, as well as Indonesia,

---

[6] The statistic $0.5 \ln[(1 + r)/(1 - r)]$ is distributed approximately normally, with a mean of $0.5 \ln[(1 + \rho)/(1 - \rho)]$ and a variance of $T - 3$ (Kendall and Stuart, 1967, pp. 292-293), where r is the estimated correlation coefficient and ρ is the null value of the correlation coefficient. Because the data for Western Europe cover a longer time span, they have a smaller variance. It turns out, however, that the critical value for the 5 percent significance level for Western Europe is almost identical to that for the 10 percent significance level for the East Asian and American data. Hence, by using a different level of significance between these two data sets, a uniform critical value of $r = 0.74$ can be employed.

[7] If the common correlation is not removed, the results indicate a very high number of significant correlations. For example, leaving aside Portugal and Switzerland, only five cross-correlations are insignificant in the whole European region. The prevalence of these positive correlations makes it difficult to make inferences about the nature of the underlying disturbances, encouraging us to prefer the normalization employed in the tables.

TABLE 2
Correlations of Growth across Different Geographic Regions

Western Europe

	Ger	Fra	Net	Bel	Den	Aus	Swi	Ita	UK	Spa	Por	Ire	Swe	Nor	Fin
Germany	1.00														
France	0.73	1.00													
Netherlands	0.78	0.80	1.00												
Belgium	0.71	0.82	0.78	1.00											
Denmark	0.66	0.55	0.63	0.47	1.00										
Austria	0.71	0.78	0.71	0.78	0.44	1.00									
Switzerland	0.55	0.62	0.55	0.60	0.28	0.62	1.00								
Italy	0.48	0.67	0.60	0.66	0.26	0.58	0.54	1.00							
United Kingdom	0.50	0.46	0.38	0.33	0.53	0.26	0.30	0.31	1.00						
Spain	0.55	0.76	0.64	0.70	0.33	0.64	0.51	0.51	0.45	1.00					
Portugal	0.55	0.69	0.56	0.64	0.34	0.63	0.61	0.63	0.50	0.52	1.00				
Ireland	0.14	0.13	0.22	0.13	-0.13	0.13	0.03	0.08	0.01	0.21	0.12	1.00			
Sweden	0.42	0.51	0.60	0.57	0.38	0.37	0.40	0.38	0.35	0.46	0.22	-0.06	1.00		
Norway	0.12	0.12	0.34	0.12	0.46	0.10	-0.05	0.26	0.05	0.05	0.01	-0.17	0.19	1.00	
Finland	0.45	0.44	0.29	0.54	0.27	0.46	0.52	0.30	0.25	0.39	0.29	-0.02	0.62	-0.05	1.00

East Asia

	Jap	Tai	Kor	Tha	HK	Sin	Mal	Ind	Phi	Aul	NZ
Japan	1.00										
Taiwan	0.62	1.00									
Korea	0.06	0.31	1.00								
Thailand	0.34	0.33	0.41	1.00							
Hong Kong	0.47	0.79	0.27	0.21	1.00						
Singapore	0.43	0.33	-0.04	0.42	0.46	1.00					
Malaysia	0.38	0.30	0.14	0.47	0.52	0.82	1.00				
Indonesia	0.13	0.41	0.13	0.36	0.42	0.47	0.49	1.00			
Philippines	0.17	0.11	0.01	0.02	0.16	0.05	0.02	-0.11	1.00		
Australia	0.41	0.28	0.16	0.30	0.16	0.02	0.20	0.08	-0.11	1.00	
New Zealand	-0.08	-0.27	-0.32	-0.19	-0.48	0.18	-0.04	-0.01	0.02	-0.31	1.00

The Americas

	US	Can	Mex	Col	Ven	Ecu	Per	Bra	Bol	Par	Uru	Arg	Chi
United States	1.00												
Canada	0.78	1.00											
Mexico	0.34	-0.01	1.00										
Colombia	0.56	0.44	0.39	1.00									
Venezuela	0.50	0.37	0.03	0.44	1.00								
Ecuador	0.53	0.28	0.51	0.47	0.47	1.00							
Peru	0.15	-0.15	0.37	0.41	0.46	0.14	1.00						
Brazil	0.42	0.12	0.38	0.61	0.34	0.58	0.51	1.00					
Bolivia	0.55	0.20	0.62	0.42	0.41	0.53	0.20	0.46	1.00				
Paraguay	0.26	-0.01	0.83	0.42	0.13	0.36	0.33	0.35	0.62	1.00			
Uruguay	0.36	0.08	0.34	0.51	0.33	0.00	0.48	0.34	0.38	0.59	1.00		
Argentina	0.30	0.17	-0.03	0.44	0.34	0.12	0.33	0.48	0.02	0.09	0.33	1.00	
Chile	0.38	0.54	0.11	0.34	-0.03	-0.18	-0.06	-0.05	0.04	0.41	0.46	0.19	1.00

TABLE 3
Correlations of Inflation across Different Geographic Regions

Western Europe

	Ger	Fra	Net	Bel	Den	Aus	Swi	Ita	UK	Spa	Por	Ire	Swe	Nor	Fin
Germany	1.00														
France	0.49	1.00													
Netherlands	0.68	0.46	1.00												
Belgium	0.57	0.67	0.64	1.00											
Denmark	0.67	0.80	0.72	0.75	1.00										
Austria	0.74	0.69	0.69	0.76	0.84	1.00									
Switzerland	0.60	0.18	0.55	0.38	0.39	0.60	1.00								
Italy	0.34	0.91	0.29	0.59	0.63	0.59	0.00	1.00							
United Kingdom	0.48	0.75	0.49	0.64	0.65	0.50	0.08	0.72	1.00						
Spain	0.28	0.77	0.33	0.58	0.64	0.57	-0.12	0.83	0.69	1.00					
Portugal	-0.07	0.60	-0.25	0.34	0.21	0.22	-0.31	0.74	0.44	0.70	1.00				
Ireland	0.49	0.80	0.60	0.55	0.72	0.60	0.23	0.69	0.68	0.60	0.33	1.00			
Sweden	0.30	0.69	0.26	0.60	0.48	0.46	0.06	0.78	0.82	0.74	0.70	0.60	1.00		
Norway	0.53	0.63	0.38	0.41	0.62	0.51	0.19	0.66	0.63	0.39	0.25	0.58	0.50	1.00	
Finland	0.37	0.66	0.51	0.73	0.73	0.69	0.29	0.63	0.60	0.53	0.30	0.46	0.49	0.47	1.00

East Asia

	Jap	Tai	Kor	Tha	HK	Sin	Mal	Ind	Phi	Aul	NZ
Japan	1.00										
Taiwan	0.81	1.00									
Korea	0.69	0.70	1.00								
Thailand	0.77	0.89	0.62	1.00							
Hong Kong	0.25	0.60	0.37	0.61	1.00						
Singapore	0.68	0.83	0.58	0.90	0.71	1.00					
Malaysia	0.50	0.54	0.37	0.63	0.66	0.63	1.00				
Indonesia	0.71	0.86	0.65	0.85	0.71	0.86	0.75	1.00			
Philippines	-0.04	-0.07	-0.22	0.10	-0.02	0.21	0.23	0.11	1.00		
Australia	0.76	0.58	0.73	0.53	0.17	0.58	0.29	0.55	-0.06	1.00	
New Zealand	-0.60	-0.33	-0.61	-0.39	0.12	-0.38	-0.20	-0.34	-0.41	-0.60	1.00

The Americas

	US	Can	Mex	Col	Ven	Ecu	Per	Bra	Bol	Par	Uru	Arg	Chi
United States	1.00												
Canada	0.90	1.00											
Mexico	-0.56	-0.64	1.00										
Colombia	0.04	-0.04	0.28	1.00									
Venezuela	0.10	-0.12	-0.02	0.22	1.00								
Ecuador	-0.32	-0.51	0.51	0.44	0.72	1.00							
Peru	-0.41	-0.50	0.22	0.29	0.67	0.81	1.00						
Brazil	-0.52	-0.63	0.46	0.35	0.60	0.87	0.96	1.00					
Bolivia	-0.49	-0.43	0.29	0.05	-0.17	0.19	0.06	0.18	1.00				
Paraguay	-0.41	-0.55	0.47	0.31	0.55	0.68	0.51	0.62	0.27	1.00			
Uruguay	-0.19	-0.26	-0.13	-0.11	0.27	0.10	0.10	0.07	0.13	0.51	1.00		
Argentina	-0.47	-0.49	0.12	0.20	0.47	0.66	0.83	0.79	0.33	0.26	0.05	1.00	
Chile	0.61	0.47	-0.51	-0.09	-0.01	-0.31	-0.46	-0.55	-0.26	-0.28	0.38	-0.37	1.00

Singapore, and Thailand exhibit significant intercountry correlations. Canadian and U.S. inflation rates are also significantly correlated, as are rates for Brazil, Ecuador, and Peru.

Speaking loosely, then, five regions displaying sympathetic co-movements in output or prices have been identified: Germany and her immediate neighbors; Japan and Taiwan; Indonesia, Singapore, and Thailand; the United States and Canada; and Brazil, Ecuador, and Peru. Whether these correlations in output and prices are consistent with correlations in underlying disturbances is the question to which we now turn.

5 ESTIMATION

Equation (4) was estimated for each of the thirty-nine countries or economies. Lags were set to two in all cases because the Schwartz-Bayes information criterion indicated that most of the models had an optimal lag length of either one or two (a uniform lag of two was chosen in order to preserve symmetry of specification across economies). Allowing for lags, the estimation period was 1963 to 1990 for the European economies and 1972 to 1989 for all Asian and American economies except Brazil and Peru. Because Brazil and Peru experienced very high inflations at the end of the period, rendering it impossible to estimate the model using data for the full period, the sample for Brazil was truncated at 1986 and the sample for Peru at 1987. (The model could be estimated for countries such as Mexico, however, in which a past high-inflation rate had declined to moderate levels by 1989.)[1]

The estimation results generally accord with the aggregate supply and demand framework of Chapter 2.[2] The over-identifying restriction that positive aggregate demand shocks should be associated with increases in prices was satisfied in thirty-six of thirty-nine cases; in three cases (Norway, the Philippines, and Uruguay) prices fell permanently in conjunction with the transitional rise in output. The price response to a supply shock was perverse in six economies (with both prices and output rising permanently). These were Hong Kong, Indonesia,

[1] We tested for structural stability around the time of the breakup of the Bretton Woods fixed-exchange-rate system and the onset of the debt crisis. For the European data, we used Chow tests to identify any changes in the structure of the vector autoregressions before and after 1971. There was no evidence in any country of a significant structural shift. For the Asian and American data, which start in 1969, we tested for breaks associated with the onset of the debt crisis in 1982. In no case was there evidence of a structural shift significant at the 1 percent level. The output equations for Argentina and Indonesia, two heavily indebted countries, showed significant breaks at the 5 percent level. The price equations for Argentina and Chile, and for Japan following its surge in inflation after the first oil shock, also show significant shifts between the two subperiods. The other eighty-nine equations for economies in Asia and the Americas appear to be stable across periods.

[2] No attempt has been made to illustrate results from individual countries. For those interested in the types of responses observed, see Stern and Bayoumi (1993), who graph responses for most OECD countries.

21

Malaysia, Norway, Singapore, and Uruguay. Three of them (Indonesia, Malaysia, and Norway) are major raw-material producers, and Hong Kong and Singapore are centers of entrepôt trade in primary commodities. As discussed earlier, for raw-material producers, supply disturbances may be closely linked to changes in the terms of trade, causing the perverse price response.

Evidence that supports this link can be found in Table 4, which shows the correlation between the estimated supply shocks and the change in the terms of trade (measured as the change in the logarithm of the ratio of the domestic-output price and the aggregate OECD price deflator, both in dollars). For the twenty industrial economies plus Korea and Taiwan, the correlations are generally small or negative, with a mean of -0.02. In contrast, the other economies in the East Asian region (with the exception of the Philippines), which show four of the six perverse price responses to supply shocks, all have large positive correlations. In Central and South America, five countries (Argentina, Bolivia, Chile, Mexico, and Peru), all of which are significant raw-material exporters, show large positive correlations, whereas the other six do not. The relatively closed nature of these economies over the sample period, and hence limited impact of changes in the terms of trade on demand, presumably explains why there are so few perverse price responses in Central and South America.

TABLE 4
CORRELATIONS OF SUPPLY DISTURBANCES WITH CHANGES IN TERMS OF TRADE

Western Europe		East Asia		The Americas	
Austria	0.09	Australia	-0.02	Canada	-0.17
Belgium	0.37	Japan	0.10	United States	-0.10
Denmark	0.08	Korea	0.01		
Finland	0.00	New Zealand	-0.32	Argentina	0.47
France	-0.10	Taiwan	-0.31	Bolivia	0.31
Germany	0.12			Brazil	0.14
Ireland	0.08	Hong Kong	0.18	Chile	0.48
Italy	-0.16	Indonesia	0.29	Colombia	0.07
Netherlands	0.04	Malaysia	0.20	Ecuador	-0.14
Norway	0.07	Philippines	0.00	Mexico	0.77
Portugal	0.32	Singapore	0.43	Paraguay	-0.17
Spain	-0.06	Thailand	0.31	Peru	0.29
Sweden	-0.14			Uruguay	-0.07
Switzerland	-0.19			Venezuela	-0.13
United Kingdom	-0.13				

6 ESTIMATION RESULTS

Correlation of Disturbances

This chapter focuses first on supply disturbances because, given the underlying model, these are unaffected by changes in demand-management policies and are more likely to be invariant with respect to alternative international monetary arrangements. Table 5 shows the correlation of supply disturbances within Europe, Asia, and the Americas, with significant correlations highlighted.[1] The results for Europe indicate that all but two of the supply shocks for Austria, Belgium, Denmark, France, Germany, and the Netherlands are significantly correlated. Switzerland's supply shocks display significant correlations with those for most of these countries as well. The six other significant positive correlations in the European bloc do not suggest a consistent regional pattern (with the exception of the positive correlation between Portugal and Spain).

The results for Asia also paint a coherent picture. Supply disturbances for Japan, Korea, and Taiwan are significantly correlated, as are those for Hong Kong, Indonesia, Malaysia, and Singapore. The only other significant positive correlation is that between Taiwan and Thailand, reflecting the intermediate position of Thailand, the supply shocks of which display large but generally insignificant correlations with those of the above seven Asian economies. Australia, New Zealand, and the Philippines have no significant positive correlations with other economies in the region. Australia and New Zealand have the only significantly negative correlation, indicating that, despite trade and investment links, these countries experience very different underlying supply disturbances.

The results for the Americas reveal only five significant positive correlations and no well-defined regional country groups. Indeed, there are eight significant negative correlations, of which two are those for the

---

[1] As with the raw data, the correlations of the G-3 countries were examined to obtain a reference value for the underlying correlations. Because these correlations were universally small, we set this value equal to zero, implying a 5 percent critical value of r = +/−0.37 for the European data and a 10 percent value of +/−0.39 for the other two regions.

TABLE 5
Correlations of Supply Disturbances across Different Geographic Regions

Western Europe

	Ger	Fra	Net	Bel	Den	Aus	Swi	Ita	UK	Spa	Por	Ire	Swe	Nor	Fin
Germany	1.00														
France	0.52	1.00													
Netherlands	0.54	0.36	1.00												
Belgium	0.62	0.40	0.56	1.00											
Denmark	0.68	0.54	0.56	0.37	1.00										
Austria	0.41	0.28	0.38	0.47	0.49	1.00									
Switzerland	0.38	0.25	0.58	0.47	0.36	0.39	1.00								
Italy	0.21	0.28	0.39	-0.00	0.15	0.06	-0.04	1.00							
United Kingdom	0.12	0.12	0.13	0.12	-0.05	-0.25	0.16	0.28	1.00						
Spain	0.33	0.21	0.17	0.23	0.22	0.25	0.07	0.20	0.01	1.00					
Portugal	0.21	0.33	0.11	0.40	-0.04	-0.03	0.13	0.22	0.27	0.51	1.00				
Ireland	-0.00	-0.21	0.11	-0.02	-0.32	0.08	0.08	0.14	0.05	-0.15	0.01	1.00			
Sweden	0.31	0.30	0.43	0.06	0.35	0.01	0.44	0.46	0.41	0.20	0.39	0.10	1.00		
Norway	-0.27	-0.11	-0.39	-0.26	-0.37	-0.21	-0.18	0.01	0.27	-0.09	0.26	0.08	0.10	1.00	
Finland	0.22	0.12	-0.25	0.06	0.30	0.11	0.06	-0.32	-0.04	0.07	-0.13	-0.23	-0.10	-0.08	1.00

East Asia

	Jap	Tai	Kor	Tha	HK	Sin	Mal	Ind	Phi	Aul	NZ
Japan	1.00										
Taiwan	0.61	1.00									
Korea	0.46	0.54	1.00								
Thailand	0.32	0.59	0.36	1.00							
Hong Kong	0.29	0.28	0.05	0.31	1.00						
Singapore	-0.10	0.25	0.02	0.29	0.63	1.00					
Malaysia	-0.02	0.06	-0.03	0.35	0.47	0.71	1.00				
Indonesia	0.14	-0.03	-0.10	0.13	0.53	0.55	0.52	1.00			
Philippines	0.10	0.37	-0.11	-0.06	0.05	0.05	-0.03	0.03	1.00		
Australia	0.12	0.21	0.19	0.14	-0.16	-0.22	0.03	0.09	0.23	1.00	
New Zealand	0.01	0.19	-0.25	0.15	-0.12	0.13	-0.11	0.01	-0.06	-0.41	1.00

The Americas

	US	Can	Mex	Col	Ven	Ecu	Per	Bra	Bol	Par	Uru	Arg	Chi
United States	1.00												
Canada	-0.47	1.00											
Mexico	-0.59	0.35	1.00										
Colombia	-0.02	0.05	0.25	1.00									
Venezuela	0.09	0.34	-0.42	0.15	1.00								
Ecuador	-0.02	0.37	0.27	0.20	0.36	1.00							
Peru	-0.40	0.05	0.37	0.07	0.10	0.28	1.00						
Brazil	0.24	0.13	-0.08	0.07	0.13	0.40	0.38	1.00					
Bolivia	-0.65	0.72	0.65	0.18	0.00	0.29	0.54	0.17	1.00				
Paraguay	-0.34	0.45	0.37	0.06	0.12	-0.07	0.16	0.22	0.39	1.00			
Uruguay	0.27	-0.31	-0.26	-0.35	0.05	-0.21	0.01	-0.06	-0.20	-0.08	1.00		
Argentina	-0.30	0.08	-0.18	0.10	0.27	-0.01	0.36	0.34	0.06	0.06	-0.48	1.00	
Chile	-0.18	0.03	0.23	0.09	-0.33	-0.41	0.19	-0.23	0.17	0.21	-0.33	0.21	1.00

United States and Canada and for the United States and Mexico. It would appear that the NAFTA countries are affected by very different supply conditions. The negative U.S.-Canadian correlation is particularly interesting because the raw data indicate that both growth and inflation are positively (and significantly) correlated—as are the demand disturbances between these two countries (see below).

To test the robustness of this result, we re-ran the model using OECD data, which covers the longer period from 1960 to 1990. Supply shocks between the United States and Canada continue to be negatively correlated over this longer period, although at –0.12, the correlation coefficient is smaller in absolute value than in the results for the shorter period.[2]

Correlation of Demand Shocks

Because demand disturbances include the impact of monetary and fiscal policies, they are less likely than supply disturbances to be informative about regional patterns. As Table 6 shows, all the regions feature a number of significant correlations, but no clear geographic pattern emerges in either Europe or the Americas. Asia, however, shows one geographic group of economies with highly correlated demand shocks, namely, Hong Kong, Indonesia, Malaysia, Singapore, and Thailand, a grouping similar to that identified by the supply disturbances.

Overall, the correlations of the estimated disturbances provide a significantly more coherent picture than the one emerging from the raw data. Three groupings are isolated that could be potential candidates for monetary unification: Germany and her Northern European neighbors; Japan, Korea, and Taiwan; and Hong Kong, Indonesia, Malaysia, and Singapore, plus (possibly) Thailand. No such groupings are apparent in the Americas. In particular, disturbances to the potential NAFTA partners tend to be negatively correlated, and the correlation of disturbances between members of MERCOSUR is small and insignificant.

---

[2] In contrast, the positive correlation between demand disturbances for the United States and Canada becomes larger when the extended data set is used. In a more detailed study focusing on NAFTA and using regional data for both the United States and Canada, we came to the same overall conclusion, namely, that the United States, Canada, and Mexico do not form a particularly homogeneous regional grouping from the point of view of macroeconomic disturbances (Bayoumi and Eichengreen, 1994a).

TABLE 6

CORRELATIONS OF DEMAND DISTURBANCES ACROSS DIFFERENT GEOGRAPHIC REGIONS

Western Europe

	Ger	Fra	Net	Bel	Den	Aus	Swi	Ita	UK	Spa	Por	Ire	Swe	Nor	Fi
Germany	1.00														
France	0.30	1.00													
Netherlands	0.21	0.34	1.00												
Belgium	0.36	0.53	0.52	1.00											
Denmark	0.34	0.32	0.20	0.30	1.00										
Austria	0.32	0.50	0.29	0.56	0.30	1.00									
Switzerland	0.18	0.42	0.37	0.28	0.22	0.45	1.00								
Italy	0.22	0.62	0.24	0.49	0.06	0.44	0.32	1.00							
United Kingdom	0.09	0.20	-0.05	-0.03	-0.00	-0.15	-0.08	0.05	1.00						
Spain	-0.10	0.53	0.11	0.26	0.25	0.30	0.04	0.43	0.23	1.00					
Portugal	0.24	0.47	0.05	0.45	0.30	0.60	0.36	0.63	0.24	0.32	1.00				
Ireland	0.06	0.09	0.39	0.00	0.34	-0.12	0.19	-0.08	0.25	0.02	-0.01	1.00			
Sweden	0.10	0.18	0.29	0.36	0.18	0.02	-0.07	0.25	0.18	-0.01	0.08	0.30	1.00		
Norway	-0.24	0.01	-0.14	-0.24	-0.11	-0.16	-0.11	-0.30	0.13	0.14	-0.19	-0.20	-0.11	1.00	
Finland	0.10	0.47	0.32	0.60	0.36	0.53	0.30	0.65	0.16	0.40	0.54	0.17	0.33	-0.21	1.00

East Asia

	Jap	Tai	Kor	Tha	HK	Sin	Mal	Ind	Phi	Aul	NZ
Japan	1.00										
Taiwan	-0.01	1.00									
Korea	0.19	0.33	1.00								
Thailand	-0.04	0.54	0.32	1.00							
Hong Kong	0.23	0.22	0.05	0.43	1.00						
Singapore	-0.09	0.44	0.27	0.70	0.37	1.00					
Malaysia	0.12	0.41	0.43	0.58	0.54	0.67	1.00				
Indonesia	0.16	0.17	0.17	0.36	0.62	0.64	0.58	1.00			
Philippines	0.29	0.09	0.16	0.15	-0.19	-0.05	-0.11	0.04	1.00		
Australia	0.22	0.20	0.46	0.32	0.32	0.34	0.50	0.05	-0.01	1.00	
New Zealand	0.00	-0.39	-0.41	0.10	0.43	0.13	0.06	0.09	-0.06	0.21	1.00

The Americas

	US	Can	Mex	Col	Ven	Ecu	Per	Bra	Bol	Par	Uru	Arg	Chi
United States	1.00												
Canada	0.30	1.00											
Mexico	-0.12	0.37	1.00										
Colombia	0.07	-0.09	-0.27	1.00									
Venezuela	0.06	0.47	0.20	0.29	1.00								
Ecuador	0.19	0.28	-0.21	0.24	0.61	1.00							
Peru	0.20	0.27	0.50	-0.33	0.05	-0.09	1.00						
Brazil	0.03	0.59	0.27	0.08	0.70	0.52	0.35	1.00					
Bolivia	0.09	0.07	0.06	-0.02	-0.20	-0.19	0.18	0.02	1.00				
Paraguay	0.11	0.50	0.23	0.39	0.51	0.13	-0.04	0.38	-0.18	1.00			
Uruguay	0.35	0.04	-0.01	0.07	-0.26	-0.45	0.25	0.24	-0.13	0.08	1.00		
Argentina	0.08	0.07	0.08	-0.08	0.35	0.29	0.35	0.15	0.01	0.33	-0.41	1.00	
Chile	0.50	0.68	0.06	0.21	0.37	0.37	-0.26	0.11	0.26	0.37	-0.24	0.05	1.00

In addition to providing estimates on the correlation of disturbances, our results also convey information about the size and the speed at which the respective economies adjust. The larger the disturbances, the more disruptive will be their effects and the greater the premium that will be placed, given any cross-country correlation, on instruments such as monetary policy) that might be used to offset them. Similarly, the slower the response of an economy to disturbances, the larger the costs of permanently fixing the exchange rate and of foregoing policy autonomy.

Because our econometric procedure restricts the variance of the estimated disturbances to unity, their magnitude can be inferred by considering the associated impulse response functions, which trace out the effect of a unit shock on prices and output. For the supply disturbances, an obvious measure is the long-run output effect, which measures the shift in potential supply (Figure 1). For demand disturbances, we calculated as a measure of size the sum of the first-year impact on output and prices, which measures the short-run change in nominal GDP.

Table 7 suggests that Europe and Asia face similarly sized supply shocks on average, whereas the Americas experience supply shocks almost twice as large. The Americas also experience relatively large demand shocks, seven times larger than Europe's and more than three times larger than Asia's. This is consistent with the greater variability of growth and (especially) inflation in the Americas.[3] There is also some evidence that the groups identified on the basis of the underlying correlations experience smaller underlying disturbances, a finding that lends further support to the viability of these regional groupings as monetary unions.

Speed of Adjustment

The speed of adjustment is summarized by the response after two years as a share of the long-run effect.[4] The second and fourth columns of Table 7 display the results. Asia has the fastest adjustment, with almost all of the change in output and prices occurring within two years. Next

---

[3] Much of this instability may reflect unstable macroeconomic policies. Correspondingly, the United States and Canada face demand disturbances the sizes of which are more akin to those in Europe than to those of the other countries in the region.

[4] Although the choice of the second year as the numerator in this calculation is somewhat arbitrary, calculations using other years produced similar results.

TABLE 7

DISTURBANCES AND ADJUSTMENT ACROSS DIFFERENT GEOGRAPHIC REGIONS

	Supply Disturbances		Demand Disturbances	
	Size	Adjustment Speed	Size	Adjustment Speed
Western Europe				
Austria	0.018	0.999	0.017	0.415
Belgium	0.028	0.668	0.020	0.508
Denmark	0.022	1.104	0.017	0.135
Finland	0.018	0.875	0.027	0.684
France	0.034	0.243	0.014	0.101
Germany	0.022	1.193	0.015	0.659
Ireland	0.021	1.222	0.038	0.382
Italy	0.030	0.427	0.036	0.380
Netherlands	0.033	0.692	0.019	0.511
Norway	0.031	0.651	0.034	0.704
Portugal	0.061	0.426	0.026	0.367
Spain	0.057	0.083	0.015	0.123
Sweden	0.030	0.261	0.012	0.419
Switzerland	0.031	0.997	0.016	0.858
United Kingdom	0.018	0.425	0.019	0.016
Average	0.030	0.684	0.022	0.417
East Asia				
Australia	0.011	0.925	0.017	0.910
Hong Kong	0.023	1.590	0.044	1.190
Indonesia	0.013	1.239	0.071	1.335
Japan	0.012	1.667	0.017	0.270
Korea	0.029	0.886	0.038	0.115
Malaysia	0.032	1.038	0.063	1.607
New Zealand	0.060	0.648	0.031	0.291
Philippines	0.089	0.587	0.081	1.475
Singapore	0.032	1.353	0.028	1.072
Taiwan	0.021	1.466	0.049	0.673
Thailand	0.026	1.381	0.042	1.279
Average	0.032	1.162	0.044	0.929
The Americas				
Argentina	0.033	1.141	0.438	1.126
Bolivia	0.069	0.585	0.636	1.302
Brazil	0.084	0.706	0.068	0.983
Canada	0.020	1.052	0.028	0.703
Chile	0.064	1.214	0.251	0.548
Colombia	0.026	0.823	0.027	0.720
Ecuador	0.162	0.402	0.076	0.987
Mexico	0.059	0.775	0.072	0.865
Paraguay	0.094	0.459	0.064	0.719
Peru	0.050	1.169	0.062	0.452
United States	0.028	0.269	0.015	0.078
Uruguay	0.049	1.014	0.074	1.227
Venezuela	0.062	0.810	0.074	0.949
Average	0.062	0.801	0.145	0.820

come the Americas, where, on average, four-fifths of adjustment is completed within two years. In Europe, by contrast, only about half of the change occurs within two years. The Northern European economies (particularly Belgium, Germany, the Netherlands, and Switzerland) are characterized by relatively rapid adjustment, whereas those of Southern Europe (Italy, Spain, and for these purposes, France) exhibit large demand disturbances and relatively slow responses. The Philippines and New Zealand and the United States and Canada appear to be less flexible than other economies in their respective regions.

Recapitulation

Chapter 2 identified three criteria (related to macroeconomic disturbances) that are useful for gauging the suitability of countries for participation in monetary unions: the size of shocks, their cross-country correlation, and the speed of domestic adjustment. All point toward three economic groupings that constitute plausible monetary unions: a Northern European bloc made up of Belgium, Denmark, France, Germany, and the Netherlands; a Northeast Asian bloc comprised of Japan, Korea, and Taiwan; and a Southeast Asian area made up of Hong Kong, Indonesia, Malaysia, Singapore, and possibly Thailand. Each of these groups is comprised of economies with relatively small disturbances, high correlations across economies, and rapid speeds of adjustment.

7   UNITED STATES REGIONAL DATA

This chapter compares the results reported above with those derived from regional data for the United States (for more detail, see Bayoumi and Eichengreen, 1993). The United States is a smoothly functioning continental monetary union with regions roughly comparable in size, in terms of population and global economic significance, to many of the countries in our sample. United States data therefore provide a useful benchmark for gauging the implications of our results for the viability of other potential monetary unions.

Data on real and nominal gross state product were collected for 1963 to 1986. These were aggregated into seven regions: New England, Mideast, Great Lakes, Plains, Southeast, Far West, and West.[1]

The over-identifying restriction regarding the simulated response of prices was satisfied for every region but the West, where supply shocks were associated with a rise in prices rather than a fall. Like most of the countries with perverse price responses to supply shocks, this region is dependent on raw-material production (especially crude oil).[2]

Table 8 reports the correlations of supply and demand disturbances for the seven U.S. regions. Six of the seven regions exhibit highly correlated supply disturbances, the exception being the West. Twelve of the fifteen cross-correlations for these regions are greater than 0.37, the significance level used in earlier analysis. Three regions, namely, New England, Mideast, and Great Lakes (the "Manufacturing Belt"), have exceptionally highly correlated supply disturbances, with higher correlations than those for any of the countries analyzed above. The other correlations are similar in magnitude to those found in the earlier analysis. By contrast, supply disturbances to the West are negatively correlated with most other regions, presumably reflecting the importance of the oil industry.

---

[1] This is in contrast to the eight regions used by the Bureau of Economic Analysis. The difference is due to our amalgamation of the smallest regions, the Rocky Mountains and the Southwest, into a combined region, which we call the "West." The Rocky Mountains and the Southwest have similar economic structures, and both specialize predominately in primary production. Together they comprise a region comparable in size to other U.S. regions and to foreign countries analyzed in this study.

[2] To determine whether the anomalous price response resulted from the aggregation of the two regions, we estimated and simulated the model separately for both and found a perverse price response to supply shocks in each case.

TABLE 8
CORRELATIONS OF DISTURBANCES ACROSS REGIONS IN THE UNITED STATES

Supply Disturbances

	New England	Mideast	Great Lakes	Southeast	Plains	Far West	West
New England	1.00						
Mideast	0.86	1.00					
Great Lakes	0.77	0.81	1.00				
Southeast	0.34	0.30	0.46	1.00			
Plains	0.44	0.67	0.66	0.49	1.00		
Far West	0.62	0.52	0.65	0.43	0.32	1.00	
West	0.07	-0.18	-0.11	-0.33	-0.66	0.26	1.00

Demand Disturbances

	New England	Mideast	Great Lakes	Southeast	Plains	Far West	West
New England	1.00						
Mideast	0.79	1.00					
Great Lakes	0.66	0.60	1.00				
Southeast	0.63	0.51	0.79	1.00			
Plains	0.51	0.50	0.70	0.69	1.00		
Far West	0.59	0.33	0.64	0.43	0.30	1.00	
West	0.26	0.28	0.03	-0.27	-0.23	0.30	1.00

The demand disturbances show a similar pattern. Correlations among the six regions other than the West are almost always significant, plausibly reflecting the effects of national macroeconomic policies, whereas correlations between the West and the rest of the country are smaller. The high cross-correlations within the United States contrast with the results reported in Table 6, consistent with our interpretation that these disturbances reflect macroeconomic policy.

Table 9 reports the size of the underlying disturbances and the speed of adjustment. The size of disturbances is similar to that found in Europe and, for the supply disturbances, Asia as well. Speeds of adjustment are comparable to those for the countries we have identified as potential participants in monetary unions.

Comparing the results for the U.S. regions with those for the potential monetary unions we have identified in Europe and East Asia, several features stand out. Most regions of the United States experience supply disturbances that are significantly more correlated than are disturbances in any of the possible monetary unions identified earlier; the correlation coefficients between the New England, Mideast, and Great Lakes regions are all over 0.75, which is higher than any of the equivalent correlations across countries. By contrast, the United States

TABLE 9
REGIONAL DISTURBANCES AND ADJUSTMENT IN THE UNITED STATES

	Supply Disturbances		Demand Disturbances	
	Size	Adjustment Speed	Size	Adjustment Speed
New England	0.032	1.149	0.015	0.433
Mideast	0.030	0.876	0.013	0.171
Great Lakes	0.040	0.630	0.030	0.050
Southeast	0.024	0.083	0.015	0.098
Plains	0.024	0.073	0.029	0.286
Far West	0.044	0.713	0.011	0.548
West	0.020	1.418	0.018	0.319
Average	0.031	0.706	0.019	0.272

also contains one region, the West, the underlying supply disturbances of which are negatively correlated with those for the rest of the country, this is not true for any of the potential unions that have been identified. Finally, U.S. regions face supply disturbances that are similar in magnitude to those faced by individual countries, and the speed of adjustment for U.S. regions is no faster than that for the countries we have identified as potential monetary-union members.

Of course, these features are not necessarily exogenous with respect to the existence of the U.S. currency union. The Northeast region of the United States has presumably become more integrated over time, and the West more specialized in raw-material production, as a result of a single currency. The speed of response to disturbances may also be affected by the inability of regions to adjust by changing the exchange rate with respect to one another. Overall, however, the results suggest that several potential monetary unions in other parts of the world are relatively similar in key respects to the U.S. currency union.

8 CONCLUSIONS

We have considered the incidence of supply and demand shocks in Western Europe, East Asia, and the Americas as a way of identifying countries experiencing similar economic disturbances and hence satisfying one of the conditions for forming an optimum currency area. To do this, we have used a procedure for recovering aggregate supply and demand disturbances from time-series data.

The results suggest the existence of three regional groupings the economies of which face similar underlying disturbances: a Northern European bloc (Austria, Belgium, Denmark, France, Germany, the Netherlands, and possibly Switzerland); a Northeast Asian bloc (Japan, Korea, and Taiwan); and a Southeast Asian bloc (Hong Kong, Indonesia, Malaysia, Singapore, and possibly Thailand). The correlations among supply shocks for these regions are not dissimilar to those found in regional data for the United States. In contrast, the United States faces very different disturbances than do Canada and Mexico, the other two countries that might conceivably join it in embracing a common currency one day. The same is true of the members of MERCOSUR.

We have further considered the size of disturbances and the speed of adjustment of the economies experiencing them. The results reinforce those derived from the correlation analysis. In Western Europe, where adjustment tends to be sluggish, implying higher costs of monetary unification, Germany and her immediate neighbors (with the notable exception of France) display the speediest responses. In Asia, where responses are faster, New Zealand and the Philippines, which both have relatively idiosyncratic disturbances, have slow responses. In the Americas, in addition to there being little correlation of supply disturbances across countries, disturbances are large, rendering the region a still less plausible candidate for monetary union. Finally, the size of disturbances and speed of adjustment of the countries we have identified (on the basis of these criteria) as plausible candidates for monetary union appear to differ little from those evident in regional data for the existing monetary union of the United States.

The potential monetary unions we have identified share several features. They tend to form contiguous geographic areas, with only a few exceptions—such as the inclusion of Hong Kong in the Southeast Asian region, although even there, all the members border a common body of

water. Germany and her neighbors, another potential grouping, have, i
addition, a history of economic integration and policy cooperation. Th
Northeast Asian bloc countries (Japan, Korea, and Taiwan) share direc
foreign-investment and component-supply links. The Southeast Asia
group members (Hong Kong, Indonesia, Malaysia, Singapore, an
Thailand) represent the next wave of Asian industrialization and contai
the region's two major financial and commercial centers.

Strikingly, these regions do not correspond closely to either curren
or prospective formal trade blocs. The region centered on German
excludes over half of the current members of the EU and includes tw
long-standing members of EFTA. Japan, Korea, and Taiwan share n
formal preferential trading arrangements. The Southeast Asian grou
excludes the Philippines, which is a member of ASEAN, and include
Hong Kong, which is not. The results indicate little similarity betwee
the disturbances experienced by the members of MERCOSUR and ar
even more negative about the suitability for monetary union of th
prospective members of NAFTA. As the example of the EU shows, thi
need not preclude these regional trading organizations from movin
toward fixed exchange rates and, ultimately, monetary union, althoug
it suggests that they will have to surmount obstacles along the way.

What do our results suggest about discussions of the scope fo
monetary union in different parts of the world? We concentrate o
Europe, the region on which much of the controversy has focused, anc
on the Americas, where regional integration initiatives have recentl
called attention to exchange-rate policy. Our results support the positio
of those (for example, Dornbusch, 1990) who have called for a two
speed monetary union in Europe—with France, Germany, and th
smaller countries of Northern Europe proceeding in the fast lane—anc
who suggest that Austria and Switzerland would also be plausibl
candidates for early participation in EMU, once Austria is admitted t
the EU, and should Switzerland choose to apply. A particularly inter
esting feature of our results, given the widespread belief that th
viability of EMU hinges on a Franco-German alliance, is the pronounce
difference in France's position in Tables 2, 3 and 5, 6. Tables 2 and 3
based on the underlying time-series data, suggest that the correlation o
French growth and inflation rates with those for other countries is ofter
higher outside than inside Northern Europe, whereas Tables 5 and 6
based on the estimated supply and demand disturbances, suggest tha
France is logically grouped with the rest of the Northern European bloc

Our results for the Americas suggest that countries in this regior
would have to undertake very major adjustments in policy anc

performance in laying the groundwork for monetary union. The negative correlation of the supply disturbances affecting the United States, on the one hand, and Canada and Mexico, on the other, is particularly striking in the context of NAFTA. On the demand side, the correlation is less pronouncedly negative for Mexico and the United States and insignificantly positive for Canada and the United States, but there, too, major shifts would have to occur with a transition to a common monetary policy. The very different aggregate supply shocks experienced by the three countries suggest that such a shift might exacerbate dislocations on the real side.[1] The results for Argentina and Chile, the aggregate supply disturbances of which are also negatively correlated with those for the United States, suggest that a future expansion of NAFTA to include South American participants does not change the picture. In Europe, it is argued that wide exchange-rate fluctuations would fan political opposition to completion of the Single Market on the grounds that some EU member states were not playing by fair monetary rules; our results suggest that the potential for exchange-rate tensions in the course of regional economic integration is even greater in the Americas.

In South America itself, trade liberalization between Argentina and Brazil has heightened tensions over exchange-rate policy. Argentine producers, living with a recently stabilized peso, complain that the rapidly depreciating Brazilian cruzeiro allows its much larger neighbor to steal an unfair competitive advantage.[2] Clearly, much of this tension reflects the very different demand disturbances afflicting the two economies (Table 6), but their supply conditions (Table 5) are also only modestly correlated, and Brazil suffers from slower adjustment of output to shocks. This suggests that a common monetary policy directed toward stabilizing the bilateral exchange rate might entail protracted adjustment problems. The low supply-side correlations are even more pronounced for the smaller MERCOSUR participants Uruguay and Paraguay.

The limitations of the analysis should be recalled. We have focused on aggregate disturbances, ignoring other factors such as the level of intraregional trade, which may also be relevant to the benefits of monetary union. And we have based inferences about the future on

---

[1] In separate work, we found that supply shocks to Western and Eastern Canada are also negatively correlated with one another, but, in those regions, extensive interregional fiscal transfers help to dissipate the resulting tensions (Bayoumi and Eichengreen, 1994a).

[2] In late 1993 and early 1994, Argentina responded to the depreciation of the cruzeiro by imposing new duties on imports of Brazilian chemicals, refrigerators, steel, paper, textiles, and agricultural machinery, thereby dealing a setback to MERCOSUR.

past data, the properties of which may not be invariant to the monetar
regime. These and other caveats notwithstanding, our analysis has clea
implications. It suggests that a European monetary union might ru
more smoothly if limited to a subset of EU members. It indicates tha
conditions are more conducive to monetary unification in East Asi
than in the Americas. And it implies that, other things being equal
ASEAN is more likely than either NAFTA or MERCOSUR to be
catalyst for negotiations to stabilize intraregional exchange rates and fo
eventual moves to establish a regional currency.

REFERENCES

Baxter, Marianne, and Alan C. Stockman, "Business Cycles and the Exchange Rate System," *Journal of Monetary Economics*, 23 (June 1989), pp. 377-400.

Bayoumi, Tamim, "The Effects of the ERM on Participating Economies," *International Monetary Fund Staff Papers*, 39 (June 1992), pp. 330-356.

Bayoumi, Tamim, and Barry Eichengreen, "Shocking Aspects of European Monetary Integration," in Francisco Torres and Francesco Giavazzi, eds., *Adjustment and Growth in the European Monetary Union*, Cambridge, Cambridge University Press, 1993, pp. 193-229.

———, "Monetary and Exchange Rate Arrangements for NAFTA," *Journal of Development Economics*, 43 (February 1994a), pp. 125-165.

———, "The Political Economy of Fiscal Restrictions: Implications for Europe from the United States," *European Economic Review*, 38 (June 1994b), pp. 783-791.

———, "Is There a Conflict Between EC Enlargement and European Monetary Unification?," *Greek Economic Review* (forthcoming 1995).

Blanchard, Olivier, and Lawrence Katz, "Regional Evolutions," *Brookings Papers on Economic Activity*, No. 2 (1992), pp. 1-61.

Blanchard, Olivier, and Danny Quah, "The Dynamic Effects of Aggregate Demand and Supply Disturbances," *American Economic Review*, 79 (September 1989), pp. 655-673.

Bryant, Ralph C., Peter Hooper, and Catherine L. Mann, eds., *Evaluating Policy Regimes: New Research in Empirical Macroeconomics*, Washington D.C., Brookings Institution, 1993.

Cohen, Daniel, and Charles Wyplosz, "The European Monetary Union: An Agnostic Evaluation," in Ralph C. Bryant, David A. Currie, Jacob A. Frenkel, Paul R. Masson, and Richard Portes, eds., *Macroeconomic Policies in an Interdependent World*, Washington D.C., Brookings Institution, 1989, pp. 311-337.

Corden, W. Max, *Monetary Integration*, Princeton Studies in International Finance No. 93, International Finance Section, Princeton, N.J., Princeton University, International Finance Section, April 1972.

De Grauwe, Paul, and Wim Vanhaverbeke, "Is Europe an Optimal Currency Area? Evidence from Regional Data," in Paul Masson and Mark Taylor, eds., *Policy Issues in the Operation of Currency Unions*, Cambridge and New York, Cambridge University Press, 1993, pp. 111-129.

Eichenbaum, Martin, and Charles Evans, "Some Empirical Evidence on the Effects of Monetary Policy Shocks on Exchange Rates," National Bureau of Economic Research Working Paper No. 4271, Cambridge, Mass., National Bureau of Economic Research, 1993.

Eichengreen, Barry, "Is Europe an Optimum Currency Area?," in Silvio Borner and Herbert Grubel, eds., *The European Community after 1992: Perspectives from the Outside*, Basingstoke, Hampshire, Macmillan, 1992, pp. 138-161.

———, "Labor Markets and European Monetary Unification," in Paul Masson and Mark Taylor, eds., *Policy Issues in the Operation of Currency Unions* Cambridge, Cambridge University Press, 1993, pp. 130-162.

———, *International Monetary Arrangements for the 21st Century*, Washington D.C., Brookings Institution, 1994.

Goto, Junichi, and Koichi Hamada, "Economic Preconditions for Asian Regional Integration," in Takatoshi Ito and Anne O. Krueger, eds., *Macroeconomic Linkage: Savings, Exchange Rates, and Capital Flows*, Chicago, University of Chicago Press for National Bureau of Economic Research, 1994, pp. 359-385.

Honkapohja, Seppo, and Pentti Pikkarainen, "Country Characteristics and the Choice of the Exchange Rate Regime: Are Mini-Skirts Followed by Maxis?," CEPR Discussion Paper No. 774, London, Centre for Economic Policy Research, December 1992.

Ishiyama, Yoshihide, "The Theory of Optimal Currency Areas: A Survey," *International Monetary Fund Staff Papers*, 22 (July 1975), pp. 344-383.

Kendall, Maurice G., and Alan Stuart, *The Advanced Theory of Statistics*, Vol 2, New York, Hafner, 1967.

Kenen, Peter B., "The Theory of Optimum Currency Areas: An Eclectic View," in Robert A. Mundell and Alexander K. Swoboda, eds., *Monetary Problems of the International Economy*, Chicago and London, University of Chicago Press, 1969, pp. 41-60.

McKinnon, Ronald I., "Optimum Currency Areas," *American Economic Review*, 53 (September 1963), pp. 717-724.

Mundell, Robert A., "A Theory of Optimum Currency Areas," *American Economic Review*, 51 (September 1961), pp. 657-664.

Organisation for Economic Co-operation and Development (OECD), *Flexibility in the Labour Market*, Paris, Organisation for Economic Co-operation and Development, 1987.

Poloz, Stephen S., "Real Exchange Rate Adjustment Between Regions in a Common Currency Area," Ottawa, Bank of Canada, 1990, processed.

Romer, Christina, and David Romer, "Does Monetary Policy Matter? A New Test in the Spirit of Friedman and Schwartz," *NBER Macroeconomics Annual* (1989), pp. 121-170.

Stern, Gabriel, and Tamim Bayoumi, "Temporary Cycles on Volatile Trends? Economic Fluctuations in 21 OECD Countries," London, Bank of England Working Paper No. 13, April 1993.

Tavlas, George S., "The 'New' Theory of Optimal Currency Areas," Washington, D.C., International Monetary Fund, 1992, processed.

orre, Augusto de la, and Margaret R. Kelly, *Regional Trade Arrangements,* Occasional Paper No. 93, Washington, D.C., International Monetary Fund, March 1992.

Veber, Axel A., "EMU and Asymmetries and Adjustment Problems in the EMS—Some Empirical Evidence," *European Economy,* Special Edition No. 1 (1991), pp. 187-207.

PUBLICATIONS OF THE
INTERNATIONAL FINANCE SECTION

Notice to Contributors

The International Finance Section publishes papers in four series: ESSAYS IN INTER-
NATIONAL FINANCE, PRINCETON STUDIES IN INTERNATIONAL FINANCE, and SPECIAL
PAPERS IN INTERNATIONAL ECONOMICS contain new work not published elsewhere.
REPRINTS IN INTERNATIONAL FINANCE reproduce journal articles previously published by Princeton faculty members associated with the Section. The Section
welcomes the submission of manuscripts for publication under the following
guidelines:

ESSAYS are meant to disseminate new views about international financial matters
and should be accessible to well-informed nonspecialists as well as to professional
economists. Technical terms, tables, and charts should be used sparingly; mathemat-
ics should be avoided.

STUDIES are devoted to new research on international finance, with preference
given to empirical work. They should be comparable in originality and technical
proficiency to papers published in leading economic journals. They should be of
medium length, longer than a journal article but shorter than a book.

SPECIAL PAPERS are surveys of research on particular topics and should be
suitable for use in undergraduate courses. They may be concerned with international
trade as well as international finance. They should also be of medium length.

Manuscripts should be submitted in triplicate, typed single sided and double
spaced throughout on 8½ by 11 white bond paper. Publication can be expedited if
manuscripts are computer keyboarded in WordPerfect 5.1 or a compatible program.
Additional instructions and a style guide are available from the Section.

How to Obtain Publications

The Section's publications are distributed free of charge to college, university, and
public libraries and to nongovernmental, nonprofit research institutions. Eligible
institutions may ask to be placed on the Section's permanent mailing list.

Individuals and institutions not qualifying for free distribution may receive all
publications for the calendar year for a subscription fee of $35.00. Late subscribers
will receive all back issues for the year during which they subscribe. Subscribers
should notify the Section promptly of any change in address, giving the old address
as well as the new.

Publications may be ordered individually, with payment made in advance. ESSAYS
and REPRINTS cost $8.00 each; STUDIES and SPECIAL PAPERS cost $11.00. An
additional $1.25 should be sent for postage and handling within the United States,
Canada, and Mexico; $1.50 should be added for surface delivery outside the region.

All payments must be made in U.S. dollars. Subscription fees and charges for
single issues will be waived for organizations and individuals in countries where
foreign-exchange regulations prohibit dollar payments.

Please address all correspondence, submissions, and orders to:

International Finance Section
Department of Economics, Fisher Hall
Princeton University
Princeton, New Jersey 08544-1021

41

List of Recent Publications

A complete list of publications may be obtained from the International Financ
Section.

ESSAYS IN INTERNATIONAL FINANCE

158. Charles E. Dumas, *The Effects of Government Deficits: A Comparativ
Analysis of Crowding Out.* (October 1985)
159. Jeffrey A. Frankel, *Six Possible Meanings of "Overvaluation": The 1981-8
Dollar.* (December 1985)
160. Stanley W. Black, *Learning from Adversity: Policy Responses to Two O
Shocks.* (December 1985)
161. Alexis Rieffel, *The Role of the Paris Club in Managing Debt Problem*
(December 1985)
162. Stephen E. Haynes, Michael M. Hutchison, and Raymond F. Mikesel
Japanese Financial Policies and the U.S. Trade Deficit. (April 1986)
163. Arminio Fraga, *German Reparations and Brazilian Debt: A Comparativ
Study.* (July 1986)
164. Jack M. Guttentag and Richard J. Herring, *Disaster Myopia in Internationa
Banking.* (September 1986)
165. Rudiger Dornbusch, *Inflation, Exchange Rates, and Stabilization.* (Octobe
1986)
166. John Spraos, *IMF Conditionality: Ineffectual, Inefficient, Mistargeted.* (De
cember 1986)
167. Rainer Stefano Masera, *An Increasing Role for the ECU: A Character i
Search of a Script.* (June 1987)
168. Paul Mosley, *Conditionality as Bargaining Process: Structural-Adjustmen
Lending, 1980-86.* (October 1987)
169. Paul A. Volcker, Ralph C. Bryant, Leonhard Gleske, Gottfried Haberle
Alexandre Lamfalussy, Shijuro Ogata, Jesús Silva-Herzog, Ross M. Star
James Tobin, and Robert Triffin, *International Monetary Cooperation: Essay
in Honor of Henry C. Wallich.* (December 1987)
170. Shafiqul Islam, *The Dollar and the Policy-Performance-Confidence Mix.* (Jul
1988)
171. James M. Boughton, *The Monetary Approach to Exchange Rates: What Nou
Remains?* (October 1988)
172. Jack M. Guttentag and Richard M. Herring, *Accounting for Losses O
Sovereign Debt: Implications for New Lending.* (May 1989)
173. Benjamin J. Cohen, *Developing-Country Debt: A Middle Way.* (May 1989)
174. Jeffrey D. Sachs, *New Approaches to the Latin American Debt Crisis.* (July 1989
175. C. David Finch, *The IMF: The Record and the Prospect.* (September 1989)
176. Graham Bird, *Loan-Loss Provisions and Third-World Debt.* (November 1989
177. Ronald Findlay, *The "Triangular Trade" and the Atlantic Economy of th
Eighteenth Century: A Simple General-Equilibrium Model.* (March 1990)
178. Alberto Giovannini, *The Transition to European Monetary Union.* (Novembe
1990)

42

79. Michael L. Mussa, *Exchange Rates in Theory and in Reality*. (December 1990)
80. Warren L. Coats, Jr., Reinhard W. Furstenberg, and Peter Isard, *The SDR System and the Issue of Resource Transfers*. (December 1990)
81. George S. Tavlas, *On the International Use of Currencies: The Case of the Deutsche Mark*. (March 1991)
82. Tommaso Padoa-Schioppa, ed., with Michael Emerson, Kumiharu Shigehara, and Richard Portes, *Europe After 1992: Three Essays*. (May 1991)
83. Michael Bruno, *High Inflation and the Nominal Anchors of an Open Economy*. (June 1991)
84. Jacques J. Polak, *The Changing Nature of IMF Conditionality*. (September 1991)
85. Ethan B. Kapstein, *Supervising International Banks: Origins and Implications of the Basle Accord*. (December 1991)
86. Alessandro Giustiniani, Francesco Papadia, and Daniela Porciani, *Growth and Catch-Up in Central and Eastern Europe: Macroeconomic Effects on Western Countries*. (April 1992)
87. Michele Fratianni, Jürgen von Hagen, and Christopher Waller, *The Maastricht Way to EMU*. (June 1992)
88. Pierre-Richard Agénor, *Parallel Currency Markets in Developing Countries: Theory, Evidence, and Policy Implications*. (November 1992)
89. Beatriz Armendariz de Aghion and John Williamson, *The G-7's Joint-and-Several Blunder*. (April 1993)
90. Paul Krugman, *What Do We Need to Know About the International Monetary System?*. (July 1993)
91. Peter M. Garber and Michael G. Spencer, *The Dissolution of the Austro-Hungarian Empire: Lessons for Currency Reform*. (February 1994)
92. Raymond F. Mikesell, *The Bretton Woods Debates: A Memoir*. (March 1994)
93. Graham Bird, *Economic Assistance to Low-Income Countries: Should the Link be Resurrected?*. (July 1994)

PRINCETON STUDIES IN INTERNATIONAL FINANCE

57. Stephen S. Golub, *The Current-Account Balance and the Dollar: 1977-78 and 1983-84*. (October 1986)
58. John T. Cuddington, *Capital Flight: Estimates, Issues, and Explanations*. (December 1986)
59. Vincent P. Crawford, *International Lending, Long-Term Credit Relationships, and Dynamic Contract Theory*. (March 1987)
60. Thorvaldur Gylfason, *Credit Policy and Economic Activity in Developing Countries with IMF Stabilization Programs*. (August 1987)
61. Stephen A. Schuker, *American "Reparations" to Germany, 1919-33: Implications for the Third-World Debt Crisis*. (July 1988)
62. Steven B. Kamin, *Devaluation, External Balance, and Macroeconomic Performance: A Look at the Numbers*. (August 1988)
63. Jacob A. Frenkel and Assaf Razin, *Spending, Taxes, and Deficits: International-Intertemporal Approach*. (December 1988)
64. Jeffrey A. Frenkel, *Obstacles to International Macroeconomic Policy Coordination*. (December 1988)

65. Peter Hooper and Catherine L. Mann, *The Emergence and Persistence of the U.S. External Imbalance, 1980-87.* (October 1989)
66. Helmut Reisen, *Public Debt, External Competitiveness, and Fiscal Discipline in Developing Countries.* (November 1989)
67. Victor Argy, Warwick McKibbin, and Eric Siegloff, *Exchange-Rate Regimes for a Small Economy in a Multi-Country World.* (December 1989)
68. Mark Gersovitz and Christina H. Paxson, *The Economies of Africa and the Prices of Their Exports.* (October 1990)
69. Felipe Larraín and Andrés Velasco, *Can Swaps Solve the Debt Crisis? Lessons from the Chilean Experience.* (November 1990)
70. Kaushik Basu, *The International Debt Problem, Credit Rationing and Loan Pushing: Theory and Experience.* (October 1991)
71. Daniel Gros and Alfred Steinherr, *Economic Reform in the Soviet Union: Pas de Deux between Disintegration and Macroeconomic Destabilization.* (November 1991)
72. George M. von Furstenberg and Joseph P. Daniels, *Economic Summit Declarations, 1975-1989: Examining the Written Record of International Cooperation.* (February 1992)
73. Ishac Diwan and Dani Rodrik, *External Debt, Adjustment, and Burden Sharing: A Unified Framework.* (November 1992)
74. Barry Eichengreen, *Should the Maastricht Treaty Be Saved?.* (December 1992)
75. Adam Klug, *The German Buybacks, 1932-1939: A Cure for Overhang?.* (November 1993)
76. Tamim Bayoumi and Barry Eichengreen, *One Money or Many? Analyzing the Prospects for Monetary Unification in Various Parts of the World.* (September 1994)

SPECIAL PAPERS IN INTERNATIONAL ECONOMICS

15. Gene M. Grossman and J. David Richardson, *Strategic Trade Policy: A Survey of Issues and Early Analysis.* (April 1985)
16. Elhanan Helpman, *Monopolistic Competition in Trade Theory.* (June 1990)
17. Richard Pomfret, *International Trade Policy with Imperfect Competition.* (August 1992)
18. Hali J. Edison, *The Effectiveness of Central-Bank Intervention: A Survey of the Literature After 1982.* (July 1993)

REPRINTS IN INTERNATIONAL FINANCE

25. Jorge Braga de Macedo, *Trade and Financial Interdependence under Flexible Exchange Rates: The Pacific Area*; reprinted from *Pacific Growth and Financial Interdependence*, 1986. (June 1986)
26. Peter B. Kenen, *The Use of IMF Credit*; reprinted from *Pulling Together: The International Monetary Fund in a Multipolar World*, 1989. (December 1989)
27. Peter B. Kenen, *Transitional Arrangements for Trade and Payments Among the CMEA Countries*; reprinted from *International Monetary Fund Staff Papers* 38 (2), 1991. (July 1991)